POPULAR SONGS

HAL LEONARD
UDENT PIANO LIBRARY

Contemporary Pop Hits

Arranged by Wendy Stevens

T0083890

CONTENTS

ISBN 978-1-4234-9952-7

HAL•LEONARD®
CORPORATION

7777 W. BLUEMOUND RD. P.O. BOX 13819 MILWAUKEE, WI 53213

Visit Hal Leonard Online at
www.halleonard.com

All the Right Moves

Words and Music by
Ryan Tedder
Arranged by Wendy Stevens

___ the right fac - es, so yeah, we're go - ing down. ___ Let's

paint the pic - ture __ of the per - fect place. __ They got it bet - er than what any - y - one's
think I'm spe - cial? _ Do you think I'm nice? _____ Am I bright e - nough to shine in your

told you. ___ They'll be the King of Hearts and you're the Queen of Spades, ____ then we'll
spac - es? ___ Be - tween the noise you hear ____ and the sound you like, ___ are we just

fight for you like we were your sol - diers. ___ I know we've got it good, but they
sink - ing in the o - cean of fac - es? ___ It can be pos - si - ble _____ that

got it made, _____ and the grass is get-ting green-er each day. _ I know things are
rain can fall _____ on - ly when it's o - ver our heads. _ The sun is shin-ing

look - ing up, _____ but soon they'll take us down be - fore an - y - bod - y's know-ing our
ev - 'ry day, _____ but it's far a - way. O - ver the world they say _

name. _ They got all the right friends in all _____ the right plac - es,
they got, they got

f

so yeah, we're go - ing down. They got all the right moves and all _

4

_____ the right fac - es, so yeah, we're go - ing down. _____ They said

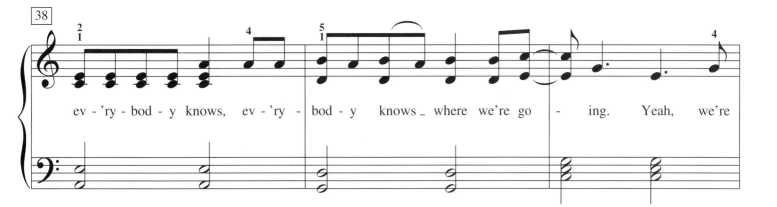

ev - 'ry - bod - y knows, ev - 'ry - bod - y knows _ where we're go - ing. Yeah, we're

go - ing down. They said ev - 'ry - bod - y knows, ev - 'ry - bod - y knows _ where we're go -

- ing. Yeah, we're go - ing down. Do you | go - ing down.

rit. _**p**_

Breakout

Words and Music by Ted Bruner,
Trey Vittetoe and Gina Schock
Arranged by Wendy Stevens

Fast Rock (♩ = 152)

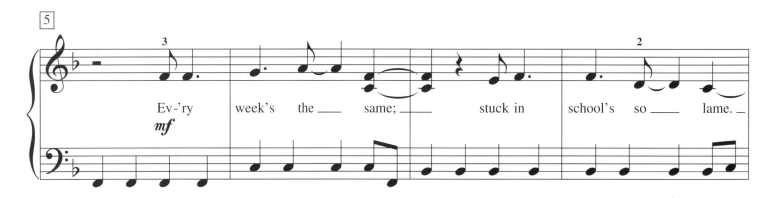

Ev-'ry week's the ___ same; ___ stuck in school's so ___ lame.

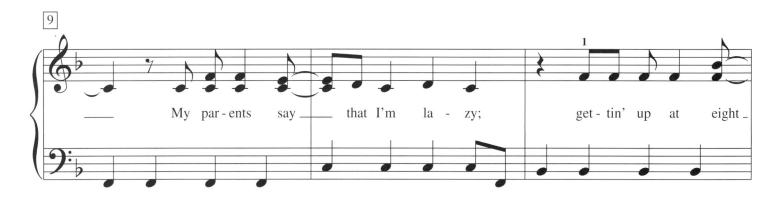

___ My par-ents say ___ that I'm la-zy; gettin' up at eight ___

___ a. m.'s cra-zy! Tired of be-in' told what to do; ___

so un-fair, __ so un-cool. __ The day's too __ long, __

__ and I'm hold-ing __ on __ till I hear the bell __ ring, __

__ 'cause that's the time when __ we're gon-na, time when __ we're gon-na

cresc.

break out; let the par-ty start. __ We're gon-na stay out, gon-na

f

break some hearts. We're gon - na dance till the dance floor falls a - part. _____

_____ Uh - oh, all o - ver a - gain. _ We're gon - na wake up ev - 'ry

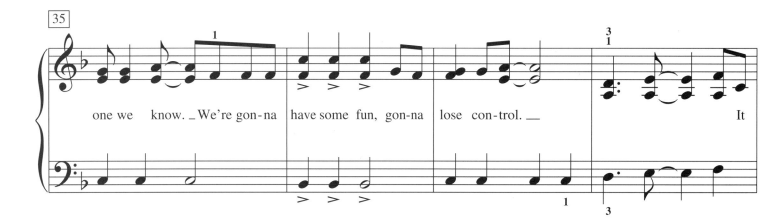

one we know. _ We're gon - na have some fun, gon - na lose con - trol. _ It

To Coda ⊕

feels so _____ good to let go, oh, _____ oh. (Go, oh, _____ oh.)
mp

Hang- in' out's just some-thing we like ___ to do; ___ my friends ___ and the

mf

mess we get in - to. These are the les - sons that ___ we ___ choose, ___

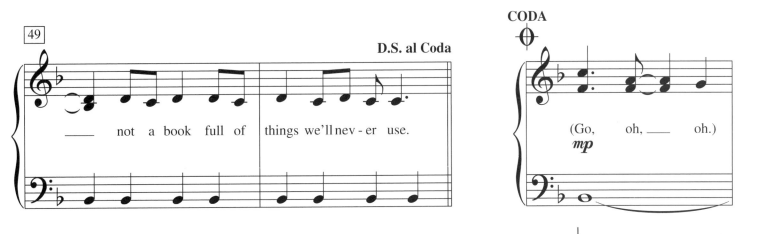

D.S. al Coda

CODA

___ not a book full of things we'll nev - er use.

(Go, oh, ___ oh.)

mp

fading away

p

Lovebug

Words and Music by Nicholas Jonas,
Joseph Jonas and Kevin Jonas II
Arranged by Wendy Stevens

Moderately fast (♩ = 152)

Called you for ___ the first ___ time yes - ter - day. ___
Fi - n'lly found ___ the miss ___ - ing part of me. ___
felt so close, ___ but you ___ were far a - way, ___

Play 3 times

I left me with - out an -

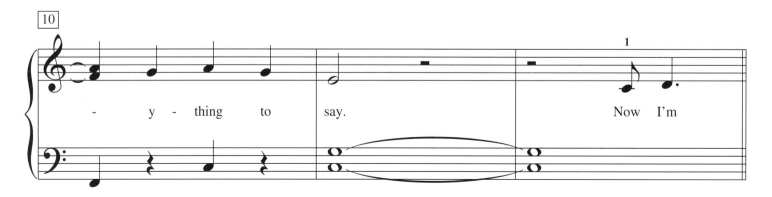

- y - thing to say. Now I'm

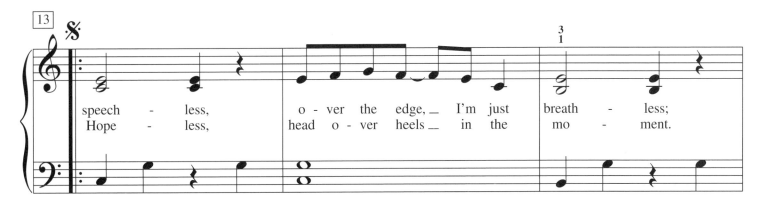

speech - less, o - ver the edge, __ I'm just breath - less;
Hope - less, head o - ver heels __ in the mo - ment.

I nev - er thought __ that I'd catch this love - bug a - gain. __
I nev - er thought __ that I'd

To Coda ⊕

get hit by this love - bug a - gain. __

I can't get ___ your smile out of my mind.

mf

mind.

I think a - bout

your eyes all the time. ___

You're beau-ti - ful, ___ but

you don't e - ven try.

Mod - es - ty _____ is just so hard to find. _____

**D.S. al Coda
(with repeat)**

CODA

Now I'm

Love Story

Words and Music by
Taylor Swift
Arranged by Wendy Stevens

you were Ro - me - o. _____ You were
you were Ro - me - o, I was the

throw - ing peb - bles, and my
scar - let let - ter and my

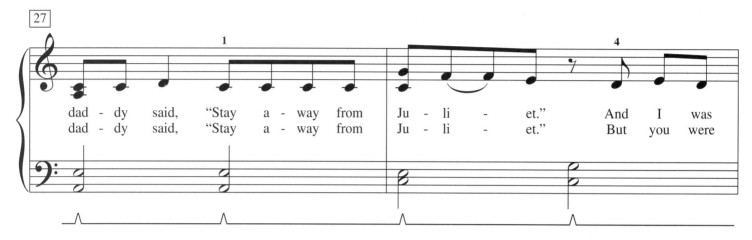

dad - dy said, "Stay a - way from
dad - dy said, "Stay a - way from

Ju - li - et." And I was
Ju - li - et." But you were

cry - in' on the stair - case, _____
ev - 'ry - thing to me. I was

beg - gin' you, "Please _____ don't go." _____
beg - gin' you, "Please _____ don't go." _____

_____∧_____ *simile*

And I _____ said, "Ro - me - o, take me

f

some-where we can be a - lone, I'll be wait - ing. All there's left to do is run.

You'll be the prince and I'll be the prin - cess. It's a love sto - ry. ___

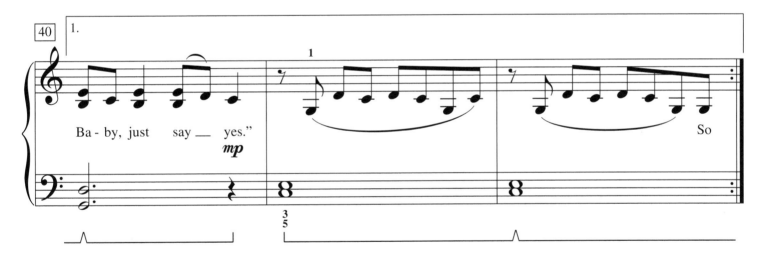

1.

Ba - by, just say ___ yes." So

2.

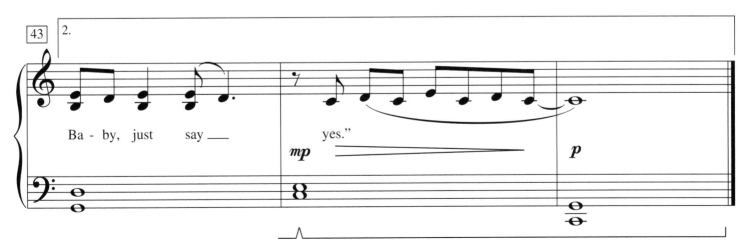

Ba - by, just say ___ yes."

When I Look at You

Words and Music by John Shanks
and Hillary Lindsey
Arranged by Wendy Stevens

Moderately, in "1" (♩ = 138)

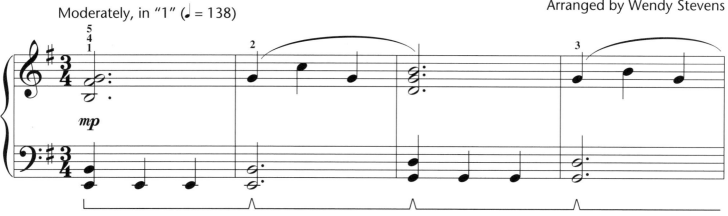

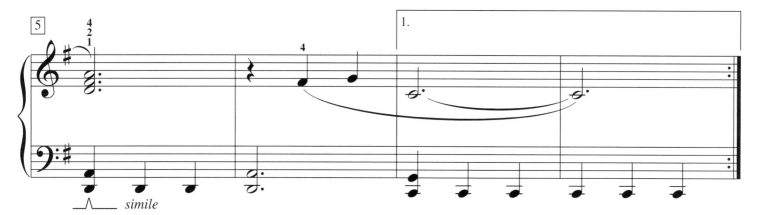

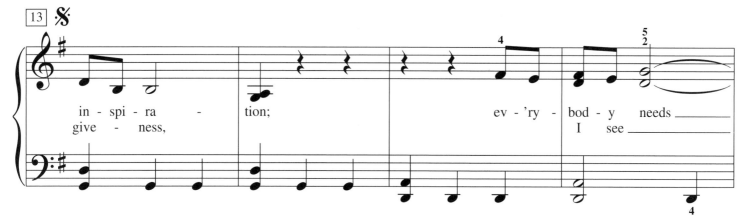

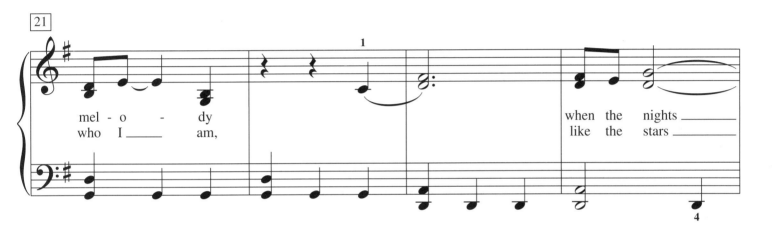

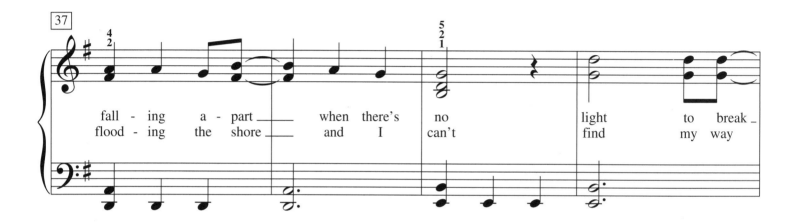

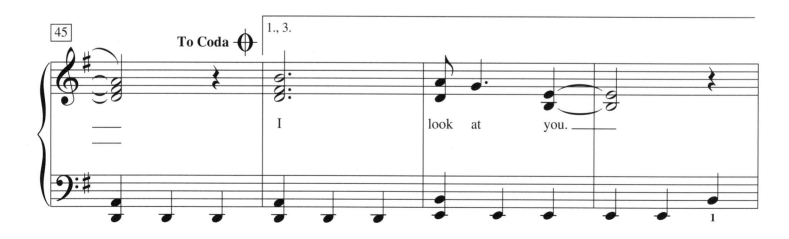

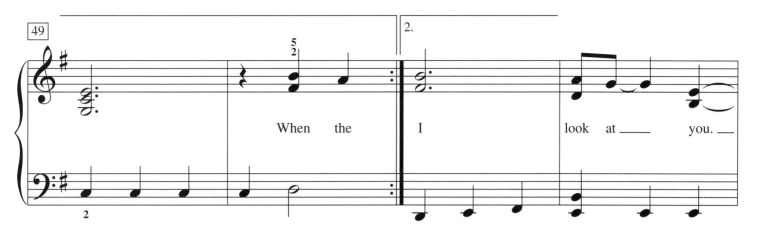

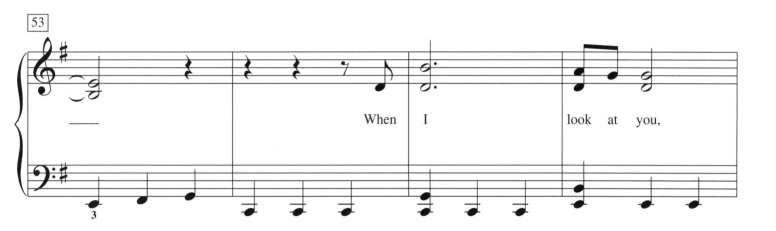

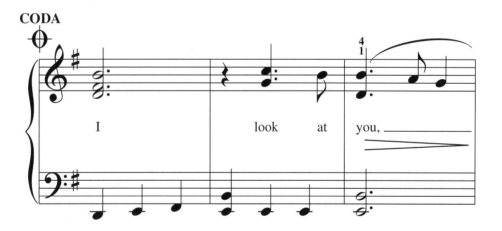

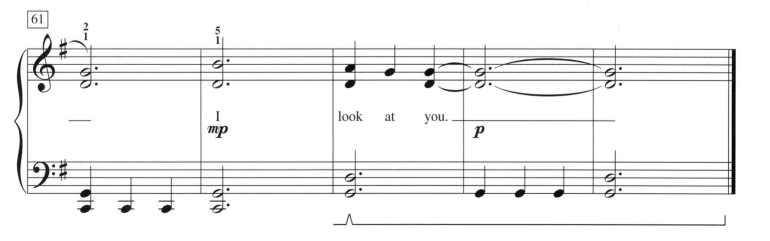

Baby

Words and Music by Justin Bieber,
Christopher Stewart, Christine Flores,
Christopher Bridges and Terius Nash
Arranged by Wendy Stevens

With energy (♩ = 132)

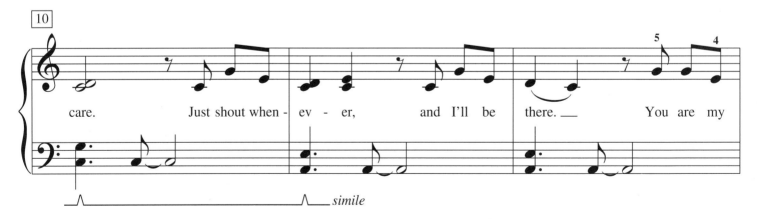

ba - by, ba - by, ba - by, oh, _____ like ba - by, ba - by, ba -

simile

- by, no, _____ like ba - by, ba - by, ba - by, oh,

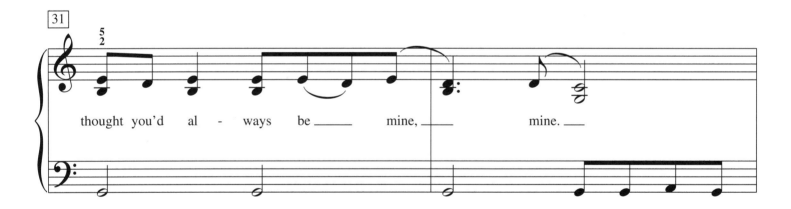

thought you'd al - ways be ____ mine, ____ mine. ____

Ba - by, ba - by, ba - by, oh, _____ like ba - by, ba - by, ba -

24

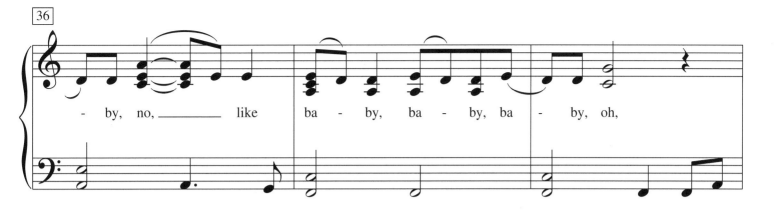

-by, no, _____ like ba - by, ba - by, ba - by, oh,

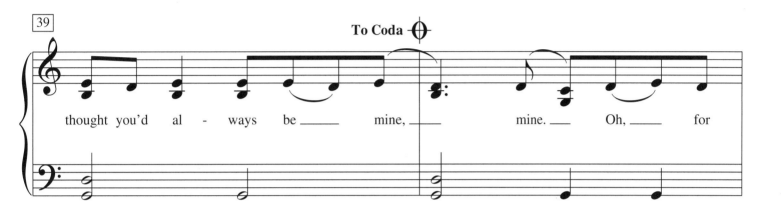

To Coda ⊕

thought you'd al - ways be _____ mine, _____ mine. _____ Oh, _____ for

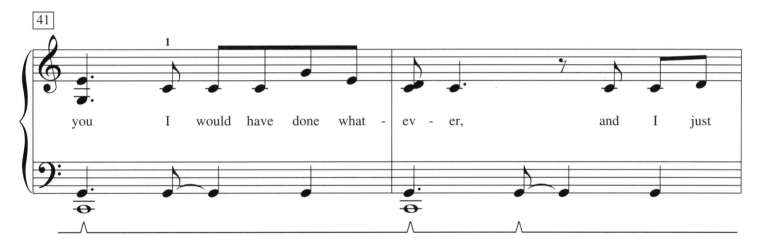

you I would have done what - ev - er, and I just

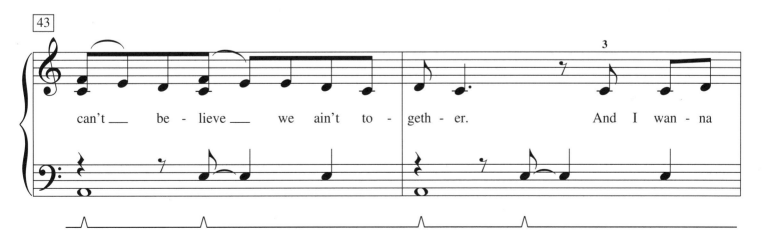

can't ___ be - lieve ___ we ain't to - geth - er. And I wan - na

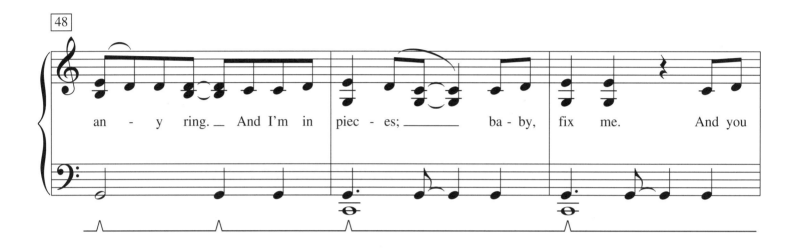

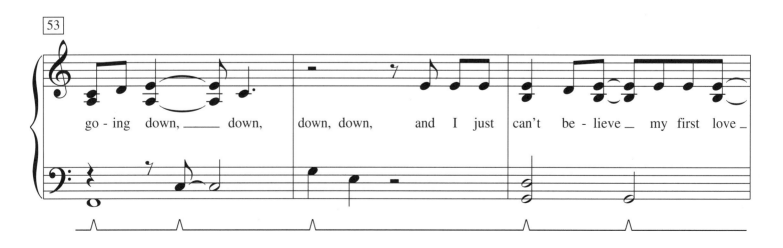

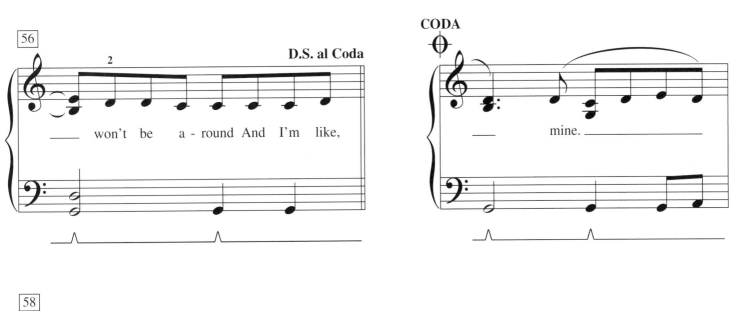

27

Hey, Soul Sister

Words and Music by Pat Monahan,
Espen Lind and Amund Bjorkland
Arranged by Wendy Stevens

Moderately (♩ = 92)

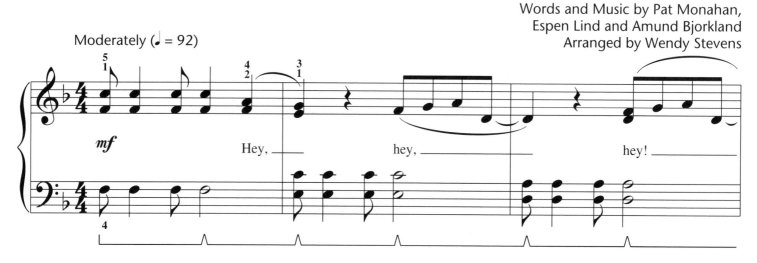

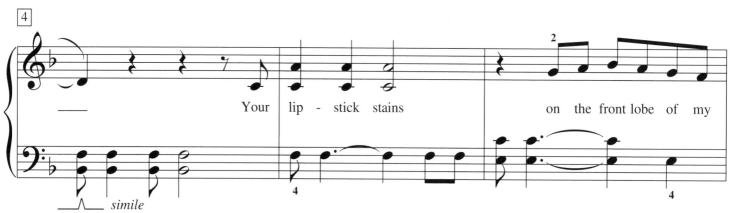

sweet moon - beam,   the smell of you in ev - ry sin - gle dream I dream, _

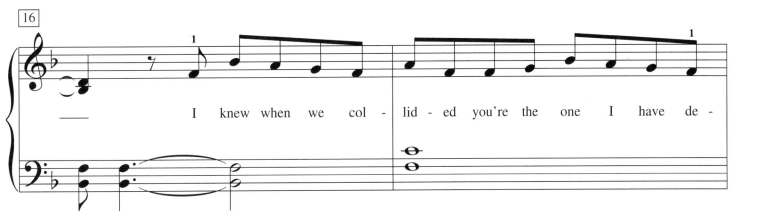

_ I knew when we col - lid - ed you're the one I have de -

cid - ed   who's one of my kind. _

Hey,   soul sis - ter, ain't _ that Mis - ter Mis - ter on the

f

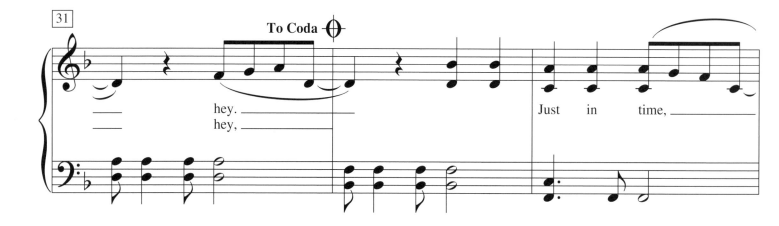

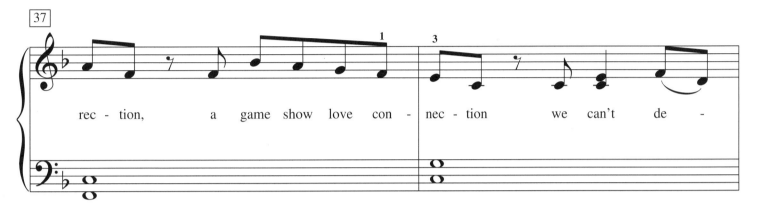

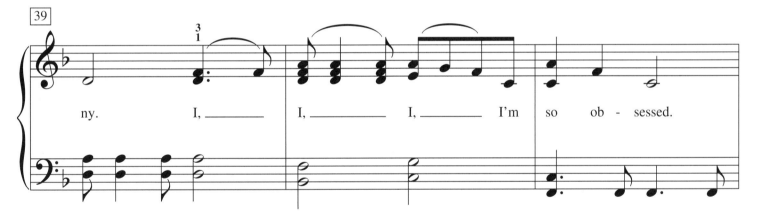

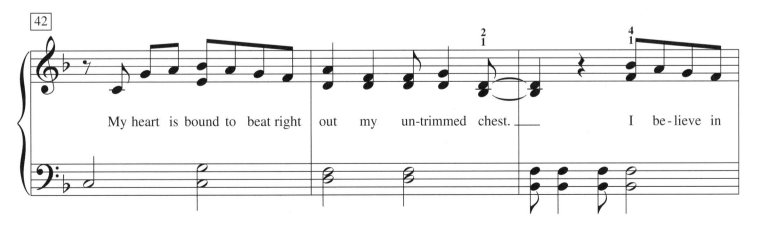

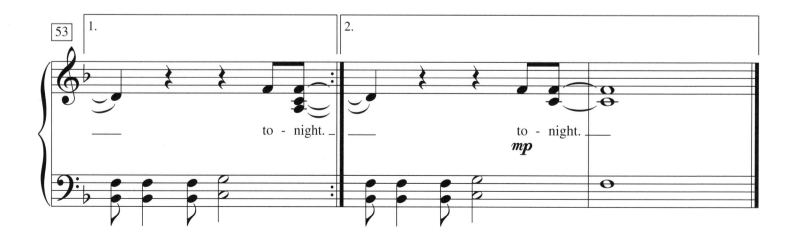